**personality profiler**

# personality profiler

*discover the real you*

**sylvia sheppard**

illustrations by cathy brear

RYLAND
PETERS
& SMALL

LONDON NEW YORK

**Designer** Luana Gobbo

**Senior Editor** Clare Double

**Production** Deborah Wehner

**Art Director** Gabriella Le Grazie

**Publishing Director** Alison Starling

**Editorial Consultant** Christina Rodenbeck

First published in the
United States in 2003
by Ryland Peters & Small, Inc.
519 Broadway, 5th Floor
New York NY 10012
www.rylandpeters.com

10 9 8 7 6 5 4 3 2 1

Text, design, and illustrations
© Ryland Peters & Small, Inc. 2003

ISBN 1 84172 522 6

Printed and bound in China

# contents

6   introduction

8   how to use this book

10   the attributes

12   the profiler

14   emotional intelligence

26   interpersonal style

40   creativity

52   cognitive style

64   acknowledgments

Hello.

I am an occupational psychologist, which means I study how people work together. My team and I wanted to make understanding personality more accessible to non-specialists— so we came up with the *Personality Profiler*.

The *Profiler* was designed using scientific principles, yet it is easy for the lay person to use. To make sure we were on the right track, we piloted the first version on a sample of respondents. Then the data was put through a considerable amount of statistical analysis in order to produce the final test. We were very pleased with the accuracy of the results.

We hope that you and your friends enjoy completing this test and are able to use the insights gained from your results beneficially.

**Sylvia Sheppard**

B.Sc. (Hons.), M.Sc. (Occ.Psych.), M.I.H.E., M.I.S.M.A., I.L.T.M.

# How to use this book

To work out how you rate on the Personality Profiler, you'll need to write down your responses to a variety of statements. You can do this in the book, but if you'd like to use the Profiler again, or with a friend, you might like to record your answers in a notebook or photocopy the relevant sections from this book.

   You'll make an analysis of your personality, divided into four main areas: Emotional Intelligence, Interpersonal Style, Creativity, and Cognitive Style. By checking your responses to a set of statements, you will build up a picture of your abilities and strengths in these areas, which are then divided into five key topics or scales (for example, under Interpersonal Style you'll see Assertiveness as one of the five). Start with whichever chapter appeals to you most; you can pick a particular section to do whenever you feel like it.

At the start of each section, there is a questionnaire made up of a list of numbered statements. Simply read each statement and put a cross in the box under the response that best suits you. For example, on page 16 the first statement is "I trust my feelings when making decisions." Would this happen "Never," "Seldom," "Sometimes," "Usually," or "Always?" Put a cross in the box that most applies to you. When you've finished, follow the simple instructions to calculate your score.

Once you have worked out your scores, read the text accompanying each key topic to find out what your results reveal about you. At the end of each of the four chapters, you will discover your total score for Emotional Intelligence, Interpersonal Style, Creativity, and Cognitive Style, and an overall summary will give you more insights.

# The attributes

**Emotional Intelligence**

This scale indicates how aware you are of your own emotions and whether you can identify and communicate them effectively to others. It also looks at how you handle others' emotions. Emotional Intelligence helps you to empathize with other people and be a good friend and coworker, and to know who you really are and what you want from life. It is the secret weapon of many successful people.

**Interpersonal Style**

Interpersonal Style measures how you relate to others: whether you're gregarious or solitary, a natural communicator or happy to stay in the background, and, most importantly, whether you are confidently assertive. This scale also examines to what degree you are prepared to get involved with others and whether you are an imaginative problem-solver or logical thinker.

## Creativity

Do you welcome new experiences, challenges, and ideas, or are you cautious about bringing change into your life? Are you a lateral or focused thinker? Your Creativity scores will bring these traits to the fore. They will also reveal how you cope with anxiety and stress and how confident you are about promoting your own ideas and talents.

## Cognitive Style

Cognitive Style is simply your favored way of thinking. This book covers five styles, and if your scores are close in all of them you're a very flexible worker. You'll probably find you score highly for one or two styles, and these—whether organized Practitioner, methodical Seeker, innovative Brainchild, flexible Team Player, or clear-sighted Referee—should ideally be appropriate for your career.

*the profiler*

*emotional
intelligence*

# Emotional Intelligence
*Questionnaire*

| | | never | seldom | some-times | usually | always |
|---|---|---|---|---|---|---|
| **1** | I trust my feelings when making decisions. | | | | ✓ | |
| **2** | I have a clear idea of my goals in life. | | | | ✓ | |
| **3** | I have a wide circle of friends. | | | | ✓ | |
| **4** | I try to make a good first impression even if I feel bad. | | | | | ✓ |
| **5** | I deal with problem issues straight away. | | | | ✓ | |
| **6** | I intuitively know when things are not right. | | | | | ✓ |
| **7** | If I feel someone deserves praise I give it. | | | | | ✓ |
| **8** | I focus easily on what really needs to be done. | | | | | ✓ |
| **9** | When I make a decision I work hard to achieve the outcome. | | | | | ✓ |
| **10** | People want me at their parties because I am fun to be with. | | | | | ✓ |
| **11** | I consider how my actions will affect others. | | | | | ✓ |
| **12** | My gut instinct about things has proved to be correct. | | | | | ✓ |
| **13** | I am able to change my mood if I really want to. | | | | | ✓ |

|  |  | never | seldom | some-times | usually | always |
|---|---|---|---|---|---|---|
| 14 | I tend to focus on the positive aspects of situations. |  |  | ✓ |  |  |
| 15 | I naturally make friends with people I work with. |  |  |  | ✓ |  |
| 16 | When I am in a new group I know how best to fit in. |  |  |  | ✓ |  |
| 17 | I treat problems as challenges that need a solution. |  |  |  |  | ✓ |
| 18 | I find I can easily sense what others are feeling. |  |  |  |  | ✓ |
| 19 | I am good at spotting relationships between people at parties. |  |  |  |  | ✓ |
| 20 | If a job does not go well, I will try again. |  |  |  |  | ✓ |

## Emotional Intelligence has five main components:

| Self-Insight | Your understanding of your own emotions. |
|---|---|
| Expressivity | Your ability to communicate and express yourself to others. |
| Sensitivity | Your understanding of, and care for, the feelings of others. |
| Drive | Your own goals and motivation to succeed. |
| Foundations | Your own emotional knowledge base and emotional style. |

Now take each cross you have entered above, find the statement numbers on the five scales on pages 18–22, and write your scores in the appropriate columns. For example, if you ticked in the far right-hand column for statement one, give yourself the five points indicated in the right-hand column of the scoring table. Each table has its own calculation instructions.

**SELF-INSIGHT: YOUR UNDERSTANDING OF YOUR OWN EMOTIONS**

| self-insight | | | | | | |
|---|---|---|---|---|---|---|
| statements | never = 1 | seldom = 2 | sometimes = 3 | usually = 4 | always = 5 | total |
| 1 | | | | | | |
| 6 | | | | | | |
| 12 | | | | | | |
| 13 | | | | | | |
| add column totals | | | | | | |
| maximum possible score for this scale | | | | | | 20 |
| your percentage score = total score ÷ maximum possible score x 100<br>so your score ÷ 20 x 100 = your percentage → | | | | | | |

A high score for Self-Insight indicates that you are not only in touch with your own emotions but can accurately identify and articulate them to others as well as yourself. You have a good understanding of the reasons behind your actions and interact well with others. In addition, because you can rationalize your feelings, you are able to cope when you are upset, angry, or sad. If you have scored low in Self-Insight, the opposite will tend to be true. A lack of understanding about your own emotions makes it difficult to cope with strong feelings, and you may well suffer from low self-esteem. In addition, you may find it difficult to control your responses in emotionally charged situations, becoming either too detached or easily devastated. This may mean that you find it hard to bounce back when you experience setbacks. Someone with low Self-Insight may find it difficult to operate in a working environment where there is a lot of conflict or pressure.

## EXPRESSIVITY: YOUR ABILITY TO COMMUNICATE AND EXPRESS YOURSELF TO OTHERS

| expressivity | | | | | | |
|---|---|---|---|---|---|---|
| statements | never = 1 | seldom = 2 | sometimes = 3 | usually = 4 | always = 5 | total |
| 3 | | | | | | |
| 7 | | | | | | |
| 10 | | | | | | |
| 15 | | | | | | |
| add column totals | | | | | | |
| maximum possible score for this scale | | | | | | 20 |
| your percentage score = total score ÷ maximum possible score x 100 so your score ÷ 20 x 100 = your percentage → | | | | | | |

A high score for Expressivity indicates that you are probably comfortable not only expressing your own emotions but handling strong emotions in others as well. Confident and in touch with your own feelings, you are not afraid to ask for help or support when you need it or to respond appropriately to emotional situations. You might be well suited to a job that involves handling people who are irrational or upset, since you would be able to communicate your own feelings appropriately. A low score for Expressivity probably means that you do not feel very happy about expressing your stronger, especially negative, feelings, and you may even avoid expressing positive feelings. You find highly expressive people very difficult to be around and your lack of expression may make you seem cold and indifferent, even though you may be very sensitive. Stifling emotions can lead to pent-up anger, sadness, and ultimately to ill-health.

## SENSITIVITY: YOUR UNDERSTANDING OF, AND CARE FOR, THE FEELINGS OF OTHERS

| sensitivity | | | | | | |
|---|---|---|---|---|---|---|
| statements | never = 1 | seldom = 2 | sometimes = 3 | usually = 4 | always = 5 | total |
| 11 | | | | | | |
| 16 | | | | | | |
| 18 | | | | | | |
| 19 | | | | | | |
| add column totals | | | | | | |
| maximum possible score for this scale | | | | | | 20 |
| your percentage score = total score ÷ maximum possible score x 100 so your score ÷ 20 x 100 = your percentage → | | | | | | |

People with a high score for Sensitivity have a good insight into the needs and feelings of others and are good judges of other people. If you scored highly here, you are the kind of person who friends go to with problems and you are a good listener. You would probably do well in a job working with others, particularly in the caring professions. You're also good at sensing the underlying motives of others and would make a good diplomat or negotiator. People with a low Sensitivity profile typically have difficulty recognizing the emotions of others and responding effectively. They tend to misread and react wrongly to the behavior of others. They also find it difficult to see a situation from another person's perspective, which can make them seem narrow-minded. Since they find it difficult to understand others, they often have trouble anticipating other people's responses and are forced to react on the spot.

## DRIVE: YOUR OWN GOALS AND MOTIVATION TO SUCCEED

| drive | | | | | | |
|---|---|---|---|---|---|---|
| statements | never = 1 | seldom = 2 | sometimes = 3 | usually = 4 | always = 5 | total |
| 4 | | | | | | |
| 9 | | | | | | |
| 17 | | | | | | |
| 20 | | | | | | |
| add column totals | | | | | | |
| maximum possible score for this scale | | | | | | 20 |
| your percentage score = total score ÷ maximum possible score x 100 so your score ÷ 20 x 100 = your percentage → | | | | | | |

If you scored highly on the Drive scale, you are likely to be highly motivated with a lot of natural enthusiasm, but be self-disciplined enough to reach your goals. Those with high Drive do not need the support of others to believe in themselves. On the other hand, those with low Drive can get overwhelmed when faced with obstacles, and easily discouraged from reaching their goals. If you had a low score, you need a lot of praise or encouragement and may lack the self-motivation to succeed in a difficult or challenging environment. You may also find it difficult to show patience when things don't happen right away, and to put aside your immediate desires for a long-term goal. Average Drive is probably enough to succeed in most things you want to do, but in the long term you may not achieve your full potential. It might be unwise to choose a career that demands high amounts of self-motivation and involves meeting tough deadlines unless you have strong Drive.

## FOUNDATIONS: YOUR OWN EMOTIONAL KNOWLEDGE BASE AND EMOTIONAL STYLE

| foundations | | | | | | |
|---|---|---|---|---|---|---|
| statements | never = 1 | seldom = 2 | sometimes = 3 | usually = 4 | always = 5 | total |
| 2 | | | | | | |
| 5 | | | | | | |
| 8 | | | | | | |
| 14 | | | | | | |
| add column totals | | | | | | |
| maximum possible score for this scale | | | | | | 20 |
| your percentage score = total score ÷ maximum possible score x 100 so your score ÷ 20 x 100 = your percentage → | | | | | | |

A high score in Foundations suggests that you have a good understanding of the principles of Emotional Intelligence and the difference it can make not only to your relationships but the way you handle yourself in everyday life. You are able to separate your own shortcomings from those of others, and consequently can cope well with failures and problems in relationships. You are able to trust yourself in decision-making, which comes from a secure base of knowing who you are and what you want out of life. A low score in Foundations suggests you lack an understanding of "emotionally smart" behavior, and consequently you often find yourself in difficulties in person-to-person dealings. You do not have the natural resources to develop your own emotional intellect and you have difficulty trusting yourself to make the right decisions in life. You are more susceptible than most to stress and worry, which in turn could have negative consequences for your health.

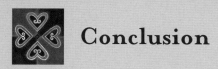

# Conclusion

**TOTAL EMOTIONAL INTELLIGENCE**

| scale | interpretation | total |
|---|---|---|
| **Self-Insight** | Your understanding of your own emotions. | |
| **Expressivity** | Your ability to communicate and express yourself to others. | |
| **Sensitivity** | Your understanding of, and care for, the feelings of others. | |
| **Drive** | Your own goals and motivation to succeed. | |
| **Foundations** | Your own emotional knowledge base and emotional style. | |
| **Add totals** | | |
| **Divide by five to find your total Emotional Intelligence Quotient:** | | |

Your score will come within one of the four bands shown right. This will give you an indication of your overall Emotional Intelligence Quotient (E.I.Q.).

| | |
|---|---|
| **20–40%** | low to poor E.I.Q. |
| **40–60%** | poor to average E.I.Q. |
| **60–80%** | average to good E.I.Q. |
| **80–100%** | good to excellent E.I.Q. |

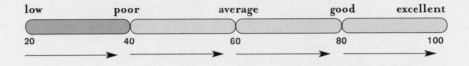

| low | poor | average | good | excellent |
|-----|------|---------|------|-----------|
| 20  | 40   | 60      | 80   | 100       |

## SUMMARY

Emotional Intelligence is frequently linked with success, not only in dealing with others but in many other areas of living. If you have a poor overall score for Emotional Intelligence, it means that you are probably not fulfilling your true potential. You do not really have the necessary knowledge and expertise to help you achieve your best in life. The good news is that there are principles of "emotionally smart" behavior, which can be learned and applied to everyday life—whatever your age. A high E.I.Q. shows that you have the skills necessary for dealing effectively with others and with your own emotional life. People with high E.I.Q.s have been shown to have stronger relationships, better health, and a more successful career, as well as other benefits. If you have scored around average, well done—you are on the way to a more emotionally intelligent lifestyle, but don't get complacent. Look at your scale scores to see which areas you could improve and think carefully about how you might put extra effort into "emotionally smart" behavior in the future.

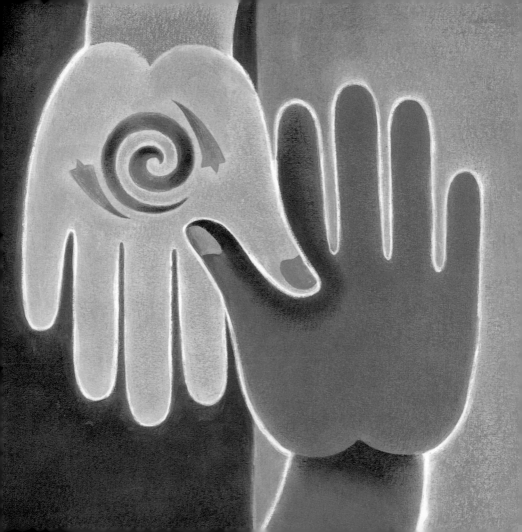

*interpersonal
style*

# Interpersonal Style
*Questionnaire*

|   |   | often | sometimes | rarely |
|---|---|---|---|---|
| 1 | Other people's problems affect me. | | | |
| 2 | I can influence others. | | | |
| 3 | I am not afraid to speak my mind. | | | |
| 4 | I can find time to help someone in need. | | | |
| 5 | I take risks to achieve change. | | | |
| 6 | I can think up solutions to problems. | | | |
| 7 | I can put my ideas across successfully to others. | | | |
| 8 | I am pretty imaginative. | | | |
| 9 | When someone is hurting, I want to help. | | | |
| 10 | I can bring people around to my way of thinking. | | | |
| 11 | I prefer variety to routine. | | | |
|   |   | agree | not sure | disagree |
| 12 | Modesty is an important quality. | | | |
| 13 | Most disputes can be sorted out amicably. | | | |
| 14 | I find it easy to consider others' ideas. | | | |
| 15 | Friends come to me with their problems. | | | |
| 16 | I feel okay standing up in front of others. | | | |

| | | agree | not sure | disagree |
|---|---|---|---|---|
| 17 | I'm often the shoulder people cry on. | | | |
| 18 | I can see another's point of view. | | | |
| 19 | My coworkers think I'm forceful. | | | |
| 20 | Making a speech is no problem. | | | |
| 21 | I can often sort out other people's problems. | | | |
| 22 | People are pretty trustworthy. | | | |
| 23 | I can cope with losing. | | | |
| 24 | Using people to get what you want is wrong. | | | |
| 25 | Appearing on stage sounds like fun. | | | |

## There are five main types of Interpersonal Style:

| | |
|---|---|
| **Communication** | Presentation and interaction skills. |
| **Sensitivity** | Awareness of others and their needs. |
| **Availability** | Hearing what others are saying, being there for others. |
| **Openness** | Acceptance of others' ideas and viewpoints, free-thinking. |
| **Assertiveness** | Getting what you want without crisis, handling conflict. |

You will find a table for each of the above five types on pages 30–37. Each table has statement numbers (from this Questionnaire) on the left, for which you can score six, three, or one. Now, with a short calculation, you have your overall score out of ten for each style scale. If you have scored above eight on any scale, this is higher than average; below four is lower than average. On page 38 you will add all five totals to find your overall Interpersonal Style profile.

## COMMUNICATION: PRESENTATION AND INTERACTION SKILLS

| communication | | | | |
|---|---|---|---|---|
| statements | left column = 6 | middle column = 3 | right column = 1 | total |
| 13 | | | | |
| 16 | | | | |
| 20 | | | | |
| 25 | | | | |
| column totals | | | | |
| add column totals to find your score: | | | | |
| calculate your total out of 10: | your score ÷ 24 x 10 = *(points out of 10)* → | | | |

If you scored high for Communication, the chances are you're happy with an audience—you may even find it exhilarating. A natural extrovert, you think social occasions are fun. You enjoy contact with others and get to know people quickly. A good talker, you know how to put across your ideas and let others know how you feel. This does not mean that you are putting on a show; your communication skills are good and your way with words means you can often influence others to agree with your way of thinking. At times, however, your ability to take control in a social setting may be seen as domineering and over-forceful. Listening can be as important as speaking! A good Communication score augurs well for a public-facing profession, work in a sales environment, teaching—or even the performing arts. A low score in Communication means you would be better described as an introvert. Quieter and more introspective, you find social occasions are more of a chore than a pleasure. It is not that you are unfriendly, however, it's just not so easy for you to put yourself forward. You also tend to keep your opinions to yourself. If you achieve an average score, you are able to handle most social situations but would not go out of your way to promote yourself.

## SENSITIVITY: AWARENESS OF OTHERS AND THEIR NEEDS

| sensitivity | | | | |
|---|---|---|---|---|
| statements | left column = 6 | middle column = 3 | right column = 1 | total |
| 1 | | | | |
| 9 | | | | |
| 12 | | | | |
| 22 | | | | |
| 23 | | | | |
| 24 | | | | |
| column totals | | | | |
| add column totals to find your score: | | | | |
| calculate your total out of 10: | your score ÷ 36 x 10 = (points out of 10) → | | | |

A high score here means you are a compassionate and understanding person. You take people at face value and are trusting of them, which means they feel valued by you. Others' feelings are important to you and you believe that cooperation is better than competition. A good listener, you are a fair judge of character and can generally trust your intuitions. You value modesty and are loath to put yourself forward, particularly at the expense of others. At times, your empathetic nature means that you are affected by others' troubles more than is necessary. A low score suggests that you are more independent and less concerned with the feelings of others. This may show in your competitive spirit. You are more skeptical about people's intentions and are not afraid to take advantage of others to get what you want. Being sensitive and amenable will make you popular, but may not help when it is time to go for promotion! An average score means you probably have a mixture of both sides. High Sensitivity is important in caring professions and managerial work—but don't be afraid to speak of your own achievements when appropriate.

## AVAILABILITY: HEARING WHAT OTHERS ARE SAYING, BEING THERE FOR OTHERS

| availability | | | | |
|---|---|---|---|---|
| statements | left column = 6 | middle column = 3 | right column = 1 | total |
| 4 | | | | |
| 15 | | | | |
| 17 | | | | |
| 18 | | | | |
| column totals | | | | |
| add column totals to find your score: | | | | |
| calculate your total out of 10: | your score ÷ 24 x 10 = *(points out of 10)* → | | | |

If you have scored highly for Availability, then chances are you are a popular person and involved with at least one other person's problems at this very moment! Your sympathetic and intuitive nature acts as a magnet to those who need support and encouragement, which you are happy to give. Your ability to listen and to see others' views in a situation makes you a good mediator, but your desire to help wherever you can could mean a tendency to become absorbed in the woes of the world. So be careful—your obliging and caring nature can be taken for granted, or you may find yourself taking on more than you can or should handle. A low score for Availability means the chances are you are more independent, with a tendency to stand back from other people's problems, and you do not like to get involved. You tend to be insular by nature and this can mean you come across as self-absorbed. You do not always realize how others feel or what impact you have on them. An average score means you are probably somewhere between both camps—you have a caring side to your nature and will get involved when and where you deem appropriate. There will, however, be times when your discretion tells you it's best to stand back and let someone else sort things out. High availability is desirable for counseling professions or mediation, where it is important that people feel comfortable in your presence, valued, and listened to. However, if you work in these areas, you must be able to separate your own feelings from those of others, so that, although you are practically involved, you do not become emotionally over-involved.

## OPENNESS: ACCEPTANCE OF OTHERS' IDEAS AND VIEWPOINTS, FREE-THINKING

| openness | | | | |
|---|---|---|---|---|
| statements | left column = 6 | middle column = 3 | right column = 1 | total |
| 6 | | | | |
| 8 | | | | |
| 11 | | | | |
| 14 | | | | |
| column totals | | | | |
| add column totals to find your score: | | | | |
| calculate your total out of 10: | your score ÷ 24 x 10 = *(points out of 10)* → | | | |

Openness is *not* the same as Availability. A high score does suggest you are flexible enough in your views to accommodate others' ideas and viewpoints easily, but this is because you are highly imaginative and receptive. You are not afraid to daydream. In fact, that is when many ideas come to you. You are innovative and can generate lots of problem-solving ideas. You are also unafraid to change your direction when needed—in fact you find it refreshing—and are not scared of taking risks. While ambiguity and uncertainty can be worrying for some, for you it means a chance to express yourself. A low score in Openness means you probably prefer routine and certainty in your working and living environments. You see daydreaming as a waste of time and are happier getting on with tasks, where you can feel satisfied that you have done a good job. You process information in a logical and sequential way and do not welcome others suggesting new angles on what you are doing! An average score means you can move in both camps. There is no right or wrong in Openness—it is just a matter of personal style. At either end of the scale you are flexible enough to cope with quite wide job demands. A high score in Openness suggests an entrepreneur, analyst, programmer, or business person, particularly if you wish to be self-employed. With a low score, you would probably be more suited to a structured job, such as a company employee, accounting, or the civil service.

## ASSERTIVENESS: GETTING WHAT YOU WANT WITHOUT CRISIS, HANDLING CONFLICT

| assertiveness | | | | |
|---|---|---|---|---|
| statements | left column = 6 | middle column = 3 | right column = 1 | total |
| 2 | | | | |
| 3 | | | | |
| 5 | | | | |
| 7 | | | | |
| 10 | | | | |
| 19 | | | | |
| 21 | | | | |
| column totals | | | | |
| add column totals to find your score: | | | | |
| calculate your total out of 10: | your score ÷ 42 x 10 = *(points out of 10)* → | | | |

A high score in Assertiveness means you probably know where you are going and how to get there. Straightforward and unafraid to make your views and feelings known, you have the diplomacy to do this without upsetting others in the process. Understanding where people are coming from enables you to give good impartial advice when needed, and your approach gets others to see things your way. You know you can be effective and dynamic without being aggressive, and expect others to treat you with the respect you show them. You have a high sense of direction and self-control and are able to face others on an even footing. Although in the other Interpersonal Styles there is no right or wrong way to do things, with Assertiveness it is hard to see the benefits of a low score. If you have scored very low for Assertiveness, you probably lack the self-confidence or control to stand up for yourself and be counted without either feeling devastated or devastating others! Low assertiveness means you are probably either too aggressive in your dealings with others, or too timid. An average score could go either way—there is nothing wrong with being forceful, but it should come from a position of self-control and confidence rather than a tendency to go in with all guns blazing every time there is a dispute. On the other hand, being timid has its own problems, and the fact that you never seem to get your voice heard can lead to disillusionment and depression. Try in future to keep yourself thinking "I'm Okay, You're Okay" when dealing with others—it really works!

# Conclusion

## INTERPERSONAL STYLE PROFILE

| scale | interpretation | total |
|---|---|---|
| **Communication** | Presentation and interaction skills. | |
| **Sensitivity** | Awareness of others and their needs. | |
| **Availability** | Hearing what others are saying, being there for others. | |
| **Openness** | Acceptance of others' ideas and viewpoints, free-thinking. | |
| **Assertiveness** | Getting what you want without crisis, handling conflict. | |

## INTERPRETING YOUR SCORE—LEVELS OF INTERPERSONAL STYLE

Look at the scale below. A total of between eight and ten for an Interpersonal Style is a high score, and you therefore probably show most of the strengths of that scale. Remember, however, that along with strengths there can be weaknesses in having a very pronounced style. If you have scored between one and three you fall into the lower-score category; these are areas that you could improve. If you have scored between four and seven, you are probably functioning at about the same level as most people.

| lower | moderate | higher |
|-------|----------|--------|
| 1 → 3 | 4 → 7 | 8 → 10 |

## SUMMARY

There are no overall rights or wrongs to Interpersonal Style—the world would be a very boring place if there were! Neither side of a spectrum is intrinsically better. Successful interpersonal life—or working life—lies in being able to display both sides of the scale spectrum at the right times. In many ways, therefore, an average score could be the most beneficial, although for some professions a more polarized scale is advantageous. The important exception is Assertiveness—as explained earlier, the ability to be truly assertive will do you nothing but good.

*creativity*

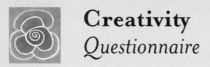

# **Creativity**
*Questionnaire*

|   |   | not like me | somewhat like me | very like me |
|---|---|---|---|---|
| 1 | I keep calm even in tense situations. | | | |
| 2 | I can take risks, even if I feel frightened. | | | |
| 3 | I like meeting new people. | | | |
| 4 | I can let ideas come to me without criticizing them. | | | |
| 5 | I am inquisitive. | | | |
| 6 | It feels comfortable keeping things the way they are. | | | |
| 7 | I usually find challenges stimulating. | | | |
| 8 | I am a creature of habit. | | | |
| 9 | Unfamiliar situations make me anxious. | | | |
| 10 | I play by the rules. | | | |
| 11 | I see myself as open-minded. | | | |
| 12 | At times I feel unable to cope. | | | |
| 13 | I find myself thinking of ways to improve things. | | | |

| | | not like me | somewhat like me | very like me |
|---|---|---|---|---|
| 14 | Sometimes you have to challenge procedures. | | | |
| 15 | I like to explore new possibilities. | | | |
| 16 | I am the one to think of unusual ways of doing things. | | | |
| 17 | I feel apprehensive and unsure of myself. | | | |
| 18 | I like to use my imagination to solve problems. | | | |
| 19 | Practical solutions are generally safest. | | | |
| 20 | I like to let my imagination go. | | | |

## Creativity is composed of five elements:

| | |
|---|---|
| **Imagination** | Your ability to think in original ways. |
| **Abstractness** | Your ability to think in abstract and creative ways. |
| **Flexibility** | Your ability to be flexible in thinking and operating. |
| **Tension/Anxiety** | How you cope with tension and anxiety. |
| **Spontaneity** | How comfortable you are about expressing yourself. |

Now take each cross you have entered above, find the statement numbers on the five scales on pages 44–48 and write your scores in the appropriate column. For example, if you ticked in the right-hand column for statement two, give yourself the six points indicated in the right-hand column of the Imagination scoring table. Each table has its own calculation instructions.

## IMAGINATION: YOUR ABILITY TO THINK IN ORIGINAL WAYS

| imagination | | | | |
|---|---|---|---|---|
| statements | not like me = 1 | somewhat like me = 3 | very like me = 6 | total |
| 2 | | | | |
| 7 | | | | |
| 11 | | | | |
| 15 | | | | |
| column totals | | | | |
| maximum possible score for this scale | | | | 24 |
| your percentage score = total score ÷ maximum possible score x 100 so your score ÷ 24 x 100 = your percentage → | | | | |

A high score for Imagination suggests that you are a very free-thinking person. New people and new situations are no problem for you. Naturally inquisitive, you find challenges stimulating and you are not afraid to question more conventional ways of thinking. A low score on Imagination, however, suggests that you are cautious about changes and challenges in your life. Although this may seem a safe option, your fear of making mistakes means you often don't give your ideas a chance. Let your imagination go a bit more and start exploring your creativity—you may even find a bit more fun in your life. An average score suggests there is no lack of creative thinking on your part, but not conforming often feels too risky and there are times when your fear of getting things wrong dampens your creative spirit. If you scored highly for Imagination, you would thrive in an environment where free-wheeling thinking and problem-solving go hand in hand—perhaps in advertising or journalism.

## ABSTRACTNESS: YOUR ABILITY TO THINK IN ABSTRACT AND CREATIVE WAYS

| abstractness | | | | |
|---|---|---|---|---|
| positive statements | not like me = 1 | somewhat like me = 3 | very like me = 6 | total |
| 13 | | | | |
| 16 | | | | |
| 18 | | | | |
| column totals | | | | |
| negative statements | not like me = 6 | somewhat like me = 3 | very like me = 1 | total |
| 19 | | | | |
| total | | | | |
| your total score for this scale is: *(positive + negative statement totals)* → | | | | |
| maximum possible score for this scale | | | | 24 |
| your percentage score = total score ÷ maximum possible score x 100 so your score ÷ 24 x 100 = your percentage → | | | | |

Scoring high in Abstractness means you might be the one your friends think a bit "off the wall" with some of your ideas. Usually the one to find the way around a problem, you are a true lateral thinker—if there is an ingenious solution somewhere, you will come up with it. Ideas come to you easily and you are prepared to consider them, however unconventional they may be, even if you make a few mistakes along the way. A low score in Abstractness means you prefer solutions to lie along safe lines. Preferring to keep your dreams within realistic boundaries, you are the tortoise who concentrates on winning the race. However, be careful, because you may miss some exciting opportunities along the way. High Abstractness will make you an excellent problem-solver and brainstormer, but beware—a regimented or tightly structured workplace may be very hard for a free-spirited thinker like you.

**FLEXIBILITY: YOUR ABILITY TO BE FLEXIBLE IN THINKING AND OPERATING**

| flexibility | | | | |
|---|---|---|---|---|
| positive statements | not like me = 1 | somewhat like me = 3 | very like me = 6 | total |
| 14 | | | | |
| total | | | | |
| negative statements | not like me = 6 | somewhat like me = 3 | very like me = 1 | total |
| 6 | | | | |
| 8 | | | | |
| 10 | | | | |
| column totals | | | | |
| your total score for this scale is: *(positive + negative statement totals)* → | | | | |
| maximum possible score for this scale | | | | 24 |
| your percentage score = total score ÷ maximum possible score x 100<br>so your score ÷ 24 x 100 = your percentage → | | | | |

A high score in Flexibility suggests a nature that is flexible and tolerant. You understand that living a creative life means taking risks and sometimes challenging conventional ways of doing things. While not necessarily impulsive, you are not afraid to bend the rules when necessary, and you take changing circumstances in your stride. A low score in Flexibility means you are more likely to be comfortable with familiar routines. Change is often threatening to you and you prefer to stick with a close circle of friends. Although you admit that improvements can be a good thing, on the whole you prefer to keep things the way they are. Unfortunately this may mean that at times you appear intolerant and inflexible. Perhaps it is time to recognize that change is a natural part of life and needn't be a bad thing. From a career perspective, a high score in Flexibility may make you an ideal "person" administrator, in personnel or recruitment.

## TENSION/ANXIETY: HOW YOU COPE WITH TENSION AND ANXIETY

| tension/anxiety | | | | |
|---|---|---|---|---|
| positive statements | not like me = 1 | somewhat like me = 3 | very like me = 6 | total |
| 1 | | | | |
| total | | | | |
| negative statements | not like me = 6 | somewhat like me = 3 | very like me = 1 | total |
| 9 | | | | |
| 12 | | | | |
| 17 | | | | |
| column totals | | | | |
| your total score for this scale is: *(positive + negative statement totals)* → | | | | |
| maximum possible score for this scale | | | | 24 |
| your percentage score = total score ÷ maximum possible score x 100 so your score ÷ 24 x 100 = your percentage → | | | | |

A high score in Tension/Anxiety and you are, conversely, a pretty unflappable person! With a relaxed personality, you are generally the one to stay unruffled when the going gets tough. Being scared does not stop you doing what you have to do, and if you get it wrong you will do better next time. Your ability to relax and switch off at the end of the day means you may well have the coping skills required for stressful professions like police or social work. A low score in Tension/Anxiety means there is a good chance that your anxieties rule your life. Though there is nothing wrong with being cautious, your frequent feelings of inadequacy in difficult situations mean you do not cope well with problems and often find yourself worrying over things. Maybe it's time you stopped being so hard on yourself, realized that everyone makes mistakes, and learned to relax a bit more.

## SPONTANEITY: HOW COMFORTABLE YOU ARE ABOUT EXPRESSING YOURSELF

| spontaneity | | | | |
|---|---|---|---|---|
| statements | not like me = 1 | somewhat like me = 3 | very like me = 6 | total |
| 3 | | | | |
| 4 | | | | |
| 5 | | | | |
| 20 | | | | |
| column totals | | | | |
| maximum possible score for this scale | | | | 24 |
| your percentage score = total score ÷ maximum possible score x 100 so your score ÷ 24 x 100 = your percentage → | | | | |

A high score in Spontaneity means you certainly could not be accused of being shy! The life and soul of the party, you love new experiences, see new possibilities where others would never have looked, and are not afraid of making a fool of yourself. Your confidence and ability to express yourself mean that your creative talents are seen in abundance. If you believe in something, it will not be long before others start believing in it too, and this skill would make you a good salesperson. A low score in Spontaneity means you are likely to be modest and unassuming by nature. There is nothing wrong with this, but perhaps it's time you started to blow your own trumpet a bit more. Then others will start seeing your creative potential, too.

# Conclusion

## TOTAL CREATIVITY SCORE

Now take the five total percentages from the above scales, enter them in this table and calculate your total Creativity score.

| scale | interpretation | total |
|---|---|---|
| **Imagination** | Your ability to think in original ways. | |
| **Abstractness** | Your ability to think in abstract and creative ways. | |
| **Flexibility** | Your ability to be flexible in thinking and operating. | |
| **Tension/Anxiety** | How you cope with tension and anxiety. | |
| **Spontaneity** | How comfortable you are about expressing yourself. | |
| **Add totals** | | |
| **Divide by five to find your total Creativity score:** | | |

Your score will come within one of the three bands indicated right. This will give you an indication of your overall Creativity.

| | |
|---|---|
| **20–40%** | low to average Creativity |
| **50–70%** | average Creativity |
| **80–100%** | average to high Creativity |

| low | | | average | | | high | | |
|---|---|---|---|---|---|---|---|---|
| 20 | 30 | 40 | 50 | 60 | 70 | 80 | 90 | 100 |

## SUMMARY

If you have scored highly in Creativity there should be no stopping you! Full of ideas and not afraid to let your imagination go, you have the self-assurance and confidence to find a way out of most tight corners, whether in the workplace or elsewhere. Your easy-going, tolerant nature makes you a popular person and your kids should never be bored—use that imagination to lift things out of the ordinary. Just remember that others have ideas too, and that sometimes two heads can be even better than one. If you have an average score for Creativity, you are undoubtedly a very expressive person. New experiences can be a pleasure to you as long as you do not find them threatening, but your anxieties about failure can sometimes get in your way. But don't worry—we can't all be designers, the world needs doers, too. If you have a low score for Creativity, the chances are you are not really fulfilling your creative potential. Maybe it is shyness or a tendency to get stuck in conventional ways of thinking, but perhaps it is time you started broadening some of your horizons and embracing more of what life has to offer. Letting yourself be more imaginative may open up some exciting possibilities. On the career front, however, you are more likely to be satisfied with routines and procedures that have proved successful in the past. Don't worry too much as long as you are happy with what you do—that is what matters most.

*cognitive style*

# Cognitive Style
*Questionnaire*

| | | very like me | somewhat like me | not like me |
|---|---|---|---|---|
| 1 | Realistic and down to earth. | | | |
| 2 | Always fair and reasonable. | | | |
| 3 | Talkative and easy to approach. | | | |
| 4 | Logical and careful. | | | |
| 5 | Composed and practical. | | | |
| 6 | I keep an objective view. | | | |
| 7 | Imaginative. | | | |
| 8 | Orderly and methodical. | | | |
| 9 | Realistically able to filter ideas. | | | |
| 10 | Need the support of others. | | | |
| | | I like | I don't mind | I don't like |
| 11 | People who put themselves forward. | | | |
| 12 | Working with others. | | | |
| 13 | Really getting down to a project. | | | |
| 14 | Unstructured working conditions. | | | |

| | | I'm at my best | I'm okay | I'm not happy |
|---|---|---|---|---|
| 15 | Having to stick to a plan. | | | |
| 16 | Putting others' ideas into practice. | | | |
| 17 | Tackling small, immediate problems. | | | |
| 18 | With easy tasks. | | | |
| 19 | Coming up with new ideas. | | | |
| 20 | Working in a team. | | | |
| 21 | With a long-term strategy. | | | |

## There are five main Cognitive Styles:

| | |
|---|---|
| **Practitioner** | Turns ideas into practical solutions, makes things happen. |
| **Seeker** | Researcher and theorizer, information-gatherer. |
| **Brainchild** | Ideas person, planner, entrepreneur, whizz-kid. |
| **Team Player** | Group worker, conciliator, bridge-builder. |
| **Referee** | Overseer, judge, regulator, director of operations. |

Now it is time to find your *preferred* Cognitive Style. You will find on pages 56–58 a table for each of the five Cognitive Styles. Each table has a series of statement numbers on the left. Where you have put a cross in the left-hand column for a statement in the Questionnaire, award yourself six points. If you have chosen the middle box, award yourself three points. If you have chosen the right-hand box, give yourself one point. Then add your column scores and turn the total scores into percentages following the instructions given on the tables.

**PRACTITIONER: TURNS IDEAS INTO PRACTICAL SOLUTIONS, MAKES THINGS HAPPEN**

| practitioner | | | | |
|---|---|---|---|---|
| statements | left column = 6 | middle column = 3 | right column = 1 | total |
| 4 | | | | |
| 9 | | | | |
| 16 | | | | |
| 21 | | | | |
| add column totals | | | | |
| maximum possible score for this scale | | | | 24 |
| your percentage score = total score ÷ maximum possible score x 100<br>so your score ÷ 24 x 100 = your percentage → | | | | |

**SEEKER: RESEARCHER AND THEORIZER, INFORMATION-GATHERER**

| seeker | | | | |
|---|---|---|---|---|
| statements | left column = 6 | middle column = 3 | right column = 1 | total |
| 1 | | | | |
| 8 | | | | |
| 13 | | | | |
| 15 | | | | |
| 17 | | | | |
| add column totals | | | | |
| maximum possible score for this scale | | | | 30 |
| your percentage score = total score ÷ maximum possible score x 100<br>so your score ÷ 30 x 100 = your percentage → | | | | |

**BRAINCHILD: IDEAS PERSON, PLANNER, ENTREPRENEUR, WHIZZ-KID**

| brainchild | | | | |
|---|---|---|---|---|
| statements | left column = 6 | middle column = 3 | right column = 1 | total |
| 7 | | | | |
| 11 | | | | |
| 14 | | | | |
| 19 | | | | |
| add column totals | | | | |
| maximum possible score for this scale | | | | 24 |
| your percentage score = total score ÷ maximum possible score x 100 so your score ÷ 24 x 100 = your percentage → | | | | |

**TEAM PLAYER: GROUP WORKER, CONCILIATOR, BRIDGE-BUILDER**

| team player | | | | |
|---|---|---|---|---|
| statements | left column = 6 | middle column = 3 | right column = 1 | total |
| 3 | | | | |
| 10 | | | | |
| 12 | | | | |
| 18 | | | | |
| 20 | | | | |
| add column totals | | | | |
| maximum possible score for this scale | | | | 30 |
| your percentage score = total score ÷ maximum possible score x 100 so your score ÷ 30 x 100 = your percentage → | | | | |

**REFEREE: OVERSEER, JUDGE, REGULATOR, DIRECTOR OF OPERATIONS**

| referee | | | | |
|---|---|---|---|---|
| statements | left column = 6 | middle column = 3 | right column = 1 | total |
| 2 | | | | |
| 5 | | | | |
| 6 | | | | |
| 16 | | | | |
| add column totals | | | | |
| maximum possible score for this scale | | | | 24 |
| your percentage score = total score ÷ maximum possible score x 100 so your score ÷ 24 x 100 = your percentage → | | | | |

Now look at your percentages for the five Cognitive Styles, and add them to this table.

| scale | interpretation | total |
|---|---|---|
| Practitioner | Turns ideas into practical solutions, makes things happen. | |
| Seeker | Researcher and theorizer, information-gatherer. | |
| Brainchild | Ideas person, planner, entrepreneur, whizz-kid. | |
| Team Player | Group worker, conciliator, bridge-builder. | |
| Referee | Overseer, judge, regulator, director of operations. | |

Which Cognitive Style have you scored highest on? This is your preferred style of thinking and working. You may well find you have scored highly for two or three other styles. These are the areas in which you are also comfortable operating. Your lowest-scoring styles are generally those ways of working that do not particularly appeal to you. Most of us will find that we are happiest in certain working roles, but this does not mean we cannot fulfill any other roles. If your scores are very close in all the style scales, you are a very flexible person indeed!

## PRACTITIONER

If you scored highest for Practitioner, you are generally the one to get things running smoothly. With your patience and realistic attitude towards possibilities, you can get the best out of a project, be it a short deadline or a long-term strategy. Your ability to cope with changed plans and sort the good from the bad means you can often see possibilities where others cannot. Although your caution, when faced with ideas, may sometimes suggest a lack of enthusiasm, once you get involved, you have the self-discipline and perseverance to see through the most challenging project. It may be others who come up with the ideas but it is often you who turns them into reality. Practitioners are able to grasp a new situation, see what needs to be done, and get on with it. Your ability to move quickly into action can often spur others to action, too. As a Practitioner, you would do well in any situation where you handle the daily prioritizing and motivation of others.

## SEEKER

The Seeker is a library of information. Logical and careful, you are the one to ask for when someone is needed for really getting down to detail. Happiest working quietly on your own, you may find the influence of others distracting rather than helpful, and this may at times make you seem a loner. Curious by nature, you love to get your teeth into a task and often will not stop until you find the answers you need. Conscientious and methodical, you are frequently a perfectionist. While this means that whatever you do is done well, it can hamper your creative abilities at times. You have a strong sense of values and are happy sticking to a plan, although on occasion your enthusiasm can lead you off on a tangent, while the overall objective has to wait! Not always recognized as an "ideas person," your ability to get to grips with and speculate about others' ideas and theories can lead to great things. With your skills, you would make a great researcher or scientist.

## BRAINCHILD

Spontaneous and full of enthusiasm, the Brainchild is at home in the company of other lively, enthusiastic people. Creative and innovative, you will consider any idea, even the most radical. Highly intuitive, you see possibilities where others have never looked, and it may be difficult for them to keep up with your imagination. You are a natural innovator, hate being restricted in your thinking, and are happiest building your own working structures. Your enthusiasm and self-confidence may seem brash at times, but you have a belief in yourself that others envy. This confidence helps you to withstand the pressure to succeed that can daunt a lesser mortal, and you thrive on new challenges and projects. Occasionally, though, you may have difficulties communicating your ideas to others. If it makes sense to you, why can't others see it? You have the ability to see things from a variety of perspectives, develop new potential, open up possibilities, and are not afraid of change. Any creative, dynamic working area would suit you.

## TEAM PLAYER

The Team Player is popular, skilled at communication, and likes working closely with others. Always fair and reasonable, you can see other points of view as well as your own, and do not mind following targets through for the good of all. Your warmth towards others is reflected in your need to have their approval and support for what you do. While others are brainstorming, you will be part of the background powerhouse that gets the work done. Approachable, easy to talk to, and good with strangers, you do not need to be the center of attention. With your nurturing nature, you find friction and conflict painful to handle, but you are very good at bridge-building and can accept differences of opinion without feeling threatened. From a working perspective, where others may need flexibility, you are comfortable knowing the boundaries of your role and responsibilities. Conscientious and tenacious, you are happiest working as part of an integrated team and would be comfortable in an organized office environment.

## REFEREE

As Referee you are happiest being in charge. Although you have a fine eye for detail, you can also keep an overall perspective in view, even when others may become sidetracked. Generally fair and reasonable, you also have a strong sense of order and propriety and may at times get frustrated with people who have a more laid-back manner. Your ability to have a clear view of targets, combined with your capacity for shaping objectives and prioritizing, will generate respect and enthusiasm from others. Generally self-confident and at times driven, when you meet problems along the way, they only spur you to greater enthusiasm to sort things out for the best. With good communication skills, you are able to bring a team together, even where there are diverse opinions. Your clarity of thinking can reaffirm directions and you are often the one to take the final decisions as well. This combination of organizational skills and a capacity to handle others would make you a great supervisor or manager—from the personnel department to the playing field!

# Conclusion

### SUMMARY

Anyone can adopt any Cognitive Style from time to time, but the styles you scored highest on are those with which you feel *most* comfortable. Of course, you may find that you take on different styles in different situations. At work or in a group setting, your style may vary depending on those around you, and you may find you can be quite flexible in how you relate to others. When considering a job, think carefully whether you would need to assume a Cognitive Style with which you can feel comfortable— for instance whether it calls for a team player or a referee.

# acknowledgments

I would like to give my utmost thanks to
Jackie Meredith who helped me develop my
initial ideas and supported me throughout
the development of this book.

# Conclusion

## SUMMARY

Anyone can adopt any Cognitive Style from time to time, but the styles you scored highest on are those with which you feel *most* comfortable. Of course, you may find that you take on different styles in different situations. At work or in a group setting, your style may vary depending on those around you, and you may find you can be quite flexible in how you relate to others. When considering a job, think carefully whether you would need to assume a Cognitive Style with which you can feel comfortable— for instance whether it calls for a team player or a referee.

# acknowledgments

I would like to give my utmost thanks to Jackie Meredith who helped me develop my initial ideas and supported me throughout the development of this book.